W9-CLH-949

Zoom in on
RESPECT FOR RULES

Rita Santos

Enslow Publishing
101 W. 23rd Street
Suite 240
New York, NY 10011
USA

enslow.com

WORDS TO KNOW

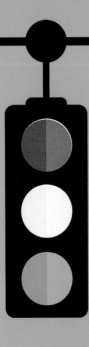

abolish To get rid of.

citizen A member of a community.

civic virtues Behaviors or habits of citizens that are good for the whole community.

consequences The things that happen because of our actions.

democracy A form of government in which all citizens have a voice.

equality Treating people the same.

federal National; having to do with the whole country.

laws Rules for citizens to follow.

moral Good and right.

petition A document that people sign when they want someone to change something.

representative A person in government who is elected to speak for the people in his or her community.

Supreme Court The highest, most powerful court in the United States.

CONTENTS

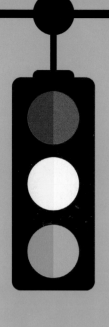

Words to Know 2

1 What Are Rules? 5

2 Why Do We Follow the Rules? 9

3 Respect for Rules at School 14

4 Citizens Respect Rules 17

Activity: A Day Without Rules..... 22

Learn More................................ 24

Index 24

Many places have rules that help keep you safe.

What Are Rules?

Rules are everywhere. Rules let us know what we should and should not do in different situations. Some rules, like don't steal, apply everywhere you go. Other rules apply only in certain places or situations. You can run in your school gym because it's safe, but running in your school hallway isn't allowed because you or someone else could get hurt.

Citizens Respect Rules

Respecting rules is a civic virtue. "Civic" means having to do with the community. A virtue is an idea or behavior that is considered good and moral. So a civic virtue is an idea or behavior that is good for the whole community. Having respect for rules is an important civic virtue. When we follow the rules, it helps keep us and others safe.

First Rules

Laws have been around for thousands of years. People in ancient Egypt probably had the first laws.

Making the Rules

It would be very hard to play a board game if all the players had a different set of rules. Following the rules makes the

6

game easier to play and more fun for everyone. As citizens, we follow a set of rules called laws. People in the government make laws according to what's best for everyone. Driving a car can be fun, but it

When we don't follow the rules, there may be a negative consequence.

can also be dangerous if you don't know what you're doing. Because of this, we have laws that say people must pass a test before they are allowed to drive. Laws like this make driving safer.

People must learn the rules of the road before they are allowed to drive.

Sometimes laws have been changed, or abolished, because they were unfair to certain groups of people. Treating everyone fairly, no matter who they are or where they come from, is known as equality. There are many laws whose goal is equality. Laws can let citizens know when they are not treating each other equally and need to change.

Why Do We Follow the Rules?

Following the rules may not sound like fun, but rules help keep things safe and fair. Games with your friends are more fun when everyone follows the rules. It's no fun when someone cheats because the game becomes unfair. Rules in the larger community work the same way.

In sports, playing fairly means following all of the rules.

Fair Rules

Some rules prevent unfairness in the community. Before 1919, women could not vote in most of America. Many people thought this was unfair because women had no say in the creation of laws that applied to them. The Supreme Court agreed that this was unfair and changed the laws to give women the right to vote.

Women marched in the early 1900s to change the voting laws.

STOP

Some rules change over time. When you were little, you slept much more often than you do now. You may not have liked your parents' rules about when you should nap, but they knew you needed rest in order to grow. As you grow, the rules about bedtime change because your need for sleep changes.

Breaking the Rules

There are consequences to breaking rules. When you don't follow the rules at home, your parents might decide to ground you or put you in time-out. While you're in a time-out, they may ask you to think about why your

Top Court

There are nine judges, or justices, on the United States Supreme Court.

12

Going to jail is a serious consequence of breaking the law.

behavior was wrong. When adults break laws, they may be put in jail. This is a place where adults are sent to think about their bad behavior. Some prisoners are allowed to leave jail early because they were very good and proved they wanted to follow the rules.

13

Respect for Rules at School

We go to school to learn. At school we have rules to help us learn. We have rules to help keep us safe. Some rules, like no talking during class, help everyone focus on their lessons. Other rules, like no name calling, make school a nicer place to be for everyone. When we all follow the rules, people are happier.

The Basics

The term "ground rules" refers to the basic rules in a game or place.

14

Classroom Rules
1. Follow the directions the first time they are given.
2. Listen carefully
3. Take care of personal belongings, other people's belongings, & school property
4. Be safe! Walk in school
5. Be kind in what you say & do
6. Work quietly. Do not disturb others.

Who Makes the Rules?

Your teacher makes the rules for your classroom. The principal makes the rules for the whole school. Your teacher and the principal want to make sure you do your best so they make rules to help guide you. School would be a much different place with no rules!

Some school rules help keep us safe. When the fire alarm

Teachers let us know what rules we need to follow in the classroom.

During a fire drill, there are special rules for what to do.

goes off, everyone has to line up and leave the building together. In case of a real fire, following these rules may help get you away from danger. Staying together helps the firemen make sure everyone has left the building.

Stay Safe

If you play sports, you may have to follow rules like wearing a helmet. Safety equipment helps protect our bodies so we can play sports without getting hurt. No one likes to get hurt. By following the rules we can help prevent injuries on our sports teams.

Citizens Respect Rules

There are two types of laws that citizens must follow: state laws and federal laws. Federal laws must be followed by all citizens, no matter where they live. Each state is also allowed to make its own rules, which are known as state laws. In California, for example, there are laws about when people can build fires outside. This is because forest fires are very easy to start in that state. Alaska does not have the same laws because forest fires are not a problem there.

Members of the United States government meet to create new laws.

Changing the Rules

Citizens can help make and change the rules in their communities. When citizens see something they would like to change, they can ask their representative to make a new law. Sometimes people will send around a petition for others to sign. If enough people sign the petition, then a change in the law could be made. Citizens can make smaller changes as well.

Rules for America

The US Constitution is a set of rules for the country. It was signed in 1787. It has had many changes, or amendments, over the years.

19

Asking your town to put a traffic light at a dangerous intersection is a small rule citizens can change in their communities.

Laws in a Democracy

In a democracy, people have a say in making laws. Sometimes citizens are asked to vote on new laws. Before we decide on a new law, we must think about how it will affect everyone. The

A woman holds a sign to show that she disagrees with new laws about immigrants.

When citizens vote, they can make their voices heard. This may mean changing unfair laws.

American government has a system of checks and balances so that unfair laws can be overturned. If a law is passed that is unfair, the Supreme Court may be asked to change it.

When everyone follows the rules it makes life safer and fairer. Good citizens follow the rules wherever they go.

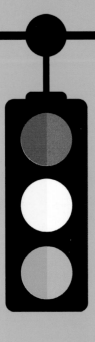

ACTIVITY: A DAY WITHOUT RULES

Rules, rules, rules! There are a lot of rules in your life. Parents, teachers, coaches, and police officers are just some of the people who expect you to follow their rules every day. Sometimes it may seem like too much. Have you ever thought about what it would be like if there were NO rules?

- Take five minutes to brainstorm as many rules as you can think of: clean your room, do your homework, raise your hand, buckle your seatbelt...these are only a few!

- Once you're done, think about your list. Now consider what life would be like without any of these rules.

- Time to get creative! Imagine you have one day with no rules. Write a story that tells what that day would be like.

- Once you've finished, think about what you've written. Would you want to live in a world with no rules? Why or why not?

LEARN MORE

Books

Coan, Sharon. *Being a Good Citizen*. Huntington Beach, CA: Teacher Created Material, 2015.

Pegis, Jessica. *What Is Citizenship?* New York, NY: Crabtree Publishing Company, 2017.

Shea, Therese M. *What Are Community Rules and Laws?* New York, NY: Britannica, 2018.

Websites

The Constitution for Kids
Usconstitution.net/constkidsK
Learn the history of the United States Constitution and Bill of Rights.

Stories About Respect
freestoriesforkids.com/tales-for-kids/values-and-virtues/stories-about-respect
Read and listen to children's stories about respect.

INDEX

civic virtue, 6
community, 6, 9, 11, 19, 20
consequences, 12–13
democracy, 20
driving, 7

equality, 8
fairness, 9, 11, 21
government, 7, 17, 19, 21
laws, 6, 7–8, 11, 17, 20–21
safety, 6, 14, 15–6, 21

school, 5, 14–16
Supreme Court, 11, 12, 21
voting, 11

Published in 2019 by Enslow Publishing, LLC.
101 W. 23rd Street, Suite 240, New York, NY 10011

Copyright © 2019 by Enslow Publishing, LLC.
All rights reserved.

No part of this book may be reproduced by any means without the written permission of the publisher.

Library of Congress Cataloging-in-Publication Data
Names: Santos, Rita, author.
Title: Zoom in on respect for rules / Rita Santos.
Description: New York : Enslow Publishing, 2019. | Series: Zoom in on civic virtues | Includes bibliographical references and index. | Audience: K-4.
Identifiers: LCCN 2017051708| ISBN 9780766097872 (library bound) | ISBN 9780766097889 (pbk.) | ISBN 9780766097896 (6 pack)
Subjects: LCSH: Civics—Juvenile literature. | Conduct of life—Juvenile literature. | Social norms—Juvenile literature.
Classification: LCC JK1759 .S334 2019 | DDC 323.6/50973—dc23
LC record available at https://lccn.loc.gov/2017051708

Printed in the United States of America

To Our Readers: We have done our best to make sure all website addresses in this book were active and appropriate when we went to press. However, the author and the publisher have no control over and assume no liability for the material available on those websites or on any websites they may link to. Any comments or suggestions can be sent by e-mail to customerservice@enslow.com.

Photos Credits: Cover, pp. 1, 8 Africa Studio/Shutterstock.com; p. 4 David Grossman/Alamy Stock Photo; p. 7 Gregory Johnston/Shutterstock.com; p. 10 Fotokostic/Shutterstock.com; p. 11 Bettmann/Getty Images; p. 13 Skyward Kick Productions/Shutterstock.com; p. 15 Dennis MacDonald/Alamy Stock Photo; p. 16 Will & Deni McIntyre/Corbis Documentary/Getty Images; p. 18 MCT/Tribune News Service/Getty Images; p. 20 Stephanie Keith/Getty Images; p. 21 Alexandru Nika/Shutterstock.com; p. 23 J.D.S/Shutterstock.com; traffic light pp. 2, 3, 22, back cover robuart/Shutterstock.com; illustrated children and teacher pp. 5, 9, 14, 17 Victor Brave/Shutterstock.com.